Contents

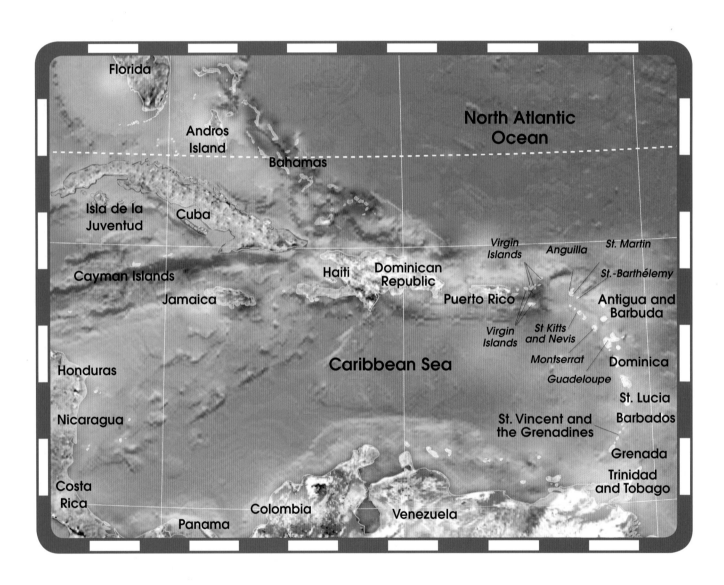

Florida

North Atlantic
Ocean

Andros
Island

Bahamas

Isla de la
Juventud

Cuba

Virgin
Islands

Anguilla

St. Martin

St.-Barthélemy

Cayman Islands

Haiti

Dominican
Republic

Jamaica

Puerto Rico

Antigua and
Barbuda

Virgin
Islands

St Kitts
and Nevis

Honduras

Caribbean Sea

Montserrat

Dominica

Guadeloupe

St. Lucia

Nicaragua

St. Vincent and
the Grenadines

Barbados

Grenada

Costa
Rica

Trinidad
and Tobago

Colombia

Venezuela

Panama

Where in the world is the Caribbean?

The Caribbean is a collection of islands found in the region south-east of North America, to the north and west of South America and east of Central America. The **archipelago** is made up of over 7000 islands stretching 4184km between Florida in the USA and Venezuela. Although they are all part of the Caribbean, each island has its own culture and traditions, so a journey through the Caribbean can be very exciting indeed. Most of the islands have people living on them. Some of the islands are owned by other countries such as Britain, France, the Netherlands and the USA. Some are even owned by very rich people, such as Little Whale Cay in the Bahamas. It is possible to rent some of these tiny islands for a holiday.

The Caribbean includes islands such as Cuba, Hispaniola, Puerto Rico, Jamaica, Trinidad, Tobago, the Bahamas, the Virgin Islands, Dominica, Antigua, St Lucia, Belize, Barbados, Haiti – and many, many more!

What is the Caribbean like?

Throughout the Caribbean there are many different types of landscapes, from **cloud forests** to volcanic mountains, **mangrove** swamps, deserts and rainforests. **Conservation International** sees the Caribbean as a hotspot for **biodiversity** – that means there are huge numbers of different types of animals and plants found there.

The Arenal volcano in Rincon de la Vieja National Park, Costa Rica, has been constantly erupting since 1968.

This sand on Pink Beach, Harbour Island, is tinted a delicate pink because it contains tiny pieces of coral.

Pink sand

The Caribbean is made up of many islands, so there is a great deal of coast to visit, with many coves and long, sandy beaches. The beautiful Pink Beach, on Harbour Island in the Bahamas, is said to be the most photographed beach in the world. In some places in the Caribbean, such as St Lucia, the sand is black as it is made from tiny pieces of volcanic lava.

Mount Roraima in Venezuela was the inspiration for Sir Arthur Conan Doyle's book The Lost World.

Big and small

Some of the islands are very tiny, such as St Martin with an area of only 96sq km. Others are much larger, such as Cuba, with an area of 110 860sq km. The population of the Caribbean tends to be concentrated on particular islands. Cuba, for example, has a population of 11 382 820. Some of the smaller islands have very few people living on them, such as Montserrat with a population of only 4000.

West Indies

Some parts of the Caribbean are called the West Indies. This is because **Christopher Columbus** (1451–1506), an Italian explorer, called the islands the Indies because he thought he had landed in India. When he realized his mistake, the name was changed to the West Indies, so people wouldn't be confused with the East Indies, now called Indonesia.

Many people holiday on cruise ships visiting the islands that make up the Caribbean.

Climate

The **climate** in most areas in the Caribbean is tropical, and as a result many beautiful and exotic plants, such as orchids, grow on the islands. A tropical climate means that you should be prepared for hot and damp conditions. You should also take plenty of high-factor sunscreen with you as the Sun is very strong. The temperature doesn't vary much between the hottest and coolest months, with temperatures of around 28°C in July to August and around 24°C in January to February. One of the reasons that the Caribbean is so popular with tourists is because there is so much sunshine, with seven to nine hours on most days.

Warm, clear water full of brightly coloured fish makes diving and snorkelling popular.

I love living in the Caribbean. After school I spend time on the beach and buy fruit and cool drinks from the beach stalls. I go snorkelling with my friends, and the water is so clear and blue it almost doesn't look real. Sometimes I feel as though I am in a wildlife documentary, as I see the coral with tiny, brightly coloured fish darting in and out. My favourite sea creatures are the rays that float about as though they are flying!
Elmino

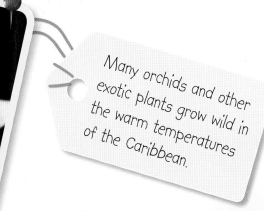

Many orchids and other exotic plants grow wild in the warm temperatures of the Caribbean.

Stormy weather

The Caribbean sometimes experiences **hurricanes**. These are terrible storms which can cause a lot of damage to property and can be dangerous to people and animals. The hurricane season is from June to November, but most hurricanes happen in September. Wind speeds during a hurricane can reach up to 240kph.

In the mountains

There is some variation in climate across the Caribbean. In Cuba and the northern islands of the Bahamas, winter temperatures sometimes fall to around 15°C, but this is still warm and pleasant. Where there are mountainous regions, such as the Blue Mountains in Jamaica, the weather can be much colder.

Hurricane Hugo caused a great deal of damage in the Caribbean in 1989.

Getting about

Once you arrive in the Caribbean there are lots of ways to travel between the islands, as many are so close together. A trip that takes in lots of different islands is often called 'island-hopping'. Some visitors to the Caribbean like to take a cruise, so they can visit many islands in one trip.

Sea and air

Regional airlines take visitors to many different islands on small planes. Some tiny planes can land on water – these are called seaplanes. The planes often fly low, so you can see the beautiful views below as you travel. There are also different types of inter-island ferries, from old-fashioned **schooners** to modern **hydrofoils** that shoot across the water at high speed.

Many people like to take sailing holidays around the Caribbean islands on schooners.

It's the school holidays and I'm having a great time visiting different islands. I have been on a beautiful old schooner, which made me feel as though I'd stepped into a film set. It was 24m long and had huge white sails which billowed in the wind. It had a diesel engine, too, in case the wind dropped! Mum and I also took a trip in a tiny seaplane. The views were amazing. We saw sharks swimming across the reef! I felt a bit worried as we landed at the quay on the tiny island, and bobbing up and down as we got off was quite scary, but it's a really fun way to travel!
Grace

Seaplanes can land on water beacuse they have special floats underneath.

Bikes are a popular way to explore many of the smaller Caribbean islands.

On your bike!

As so many of the islands are small, the local people get around on mopeds and bikes, as well as by using cars. If you visit a Caribbean island, you can often hire mountain bikes from larger hotels. This is a great way to see the sights and keep fit at the same time. Larger islands have good bus networks, especially in the cities. Riding on the buses means you can meet the local people as you travel – though the buses do get very full.

Major cities

Although visitors tend to come to the Caribbean for the spectacular beaches, the stunning scenery and the glorious weather, there are also some interesting towns and cities to explore. Kingston is the capital of Jamaica. It has two areas: Downtown, which is the oldest part of Kingston and which has many historic buildings, and New Kingston, with visitor attractions such as the Bob Marley Museum. Bob Marley was one of the world's most popular **reggae** artists, and the museum is the house in which he lived when he was alive.

Port Royal was known as the 'richest and wickedest city on Earth' because it was a safe place for pirates to hide after they had attacked a ship.

Old capital

Port Royal was Jamaica's previous capital city, and was on the top of the **peninsula** that borders the harbour. A museum there tells the story of how Port Royal was submerged under the sea after an earthquake in 1692.

The Bob Marley Museum is in the house where the musician lived and founded a record label called Tuff Gong along with his band called The Wailers.

Historical place

Santo Domingo in the Dominican Republic is a beautiful, historic city. Many buildings there date from the 1500s, including the Cathedral Basilica Santa Maria la Menor. Visitors also love the dance clubs where they can **merengue** and **salsa**. One of the most impressive clubs is the Guácara Taina, which is in a massive, natural underground cave.

This club is in a cave 15m below the ground.

The original Santo Domingo was a walled city that is now part of the larger modern city.

Beautiful gardens

The Hope Botanical Gardens in Kingston are a lovely place to visit, and you can see many beautiful orchids growing there. You should also visit the White Marl Arawak Museum where you can see **artefacts** from the ancient culture of the Arawak Indians, who were first people to live in Jamaica.

We went to the Hope Botanical Gardens today. There were orchids growing wild just like the pink ones Granny grows as houseplants. I learnt that **crops** such as pineapple, **cocoa** and coffee were introduced to Jamaica by being first grown in the gardens.
Love Sam

Farming

As the Caribbean islands are so warm, farmers can grow a huge variety of crops, both for local people to eat fresh and for **export**. Crops grown for the local people to eat include yams, avocados, pumpkins and peppers. Food grown for export include bananas, sugar, coffee, cocoa, oranges, grapefruits, tangerines, coconuts and spices, such as pimento, from which the seasoning allspice is made.

Sweet potatoes

Avocados

Fruit and vegetables grown in the Caribbean are flown all over the world to be sold in shops and supermarkets.

Sweet peppers

Pumpkins

At school this week, we learned about Fairtrade projects. We were all really interested in how Fairtrade chocolate is made. I didn't realize that so many cocoa farmers around the world were so poor. We found out that you can now buy chocolate, drinking chocolate and cocoa that has been grown and produced in fair circumstances, which means the farmers are paid a fair price for their cocoa beans.
Ruby

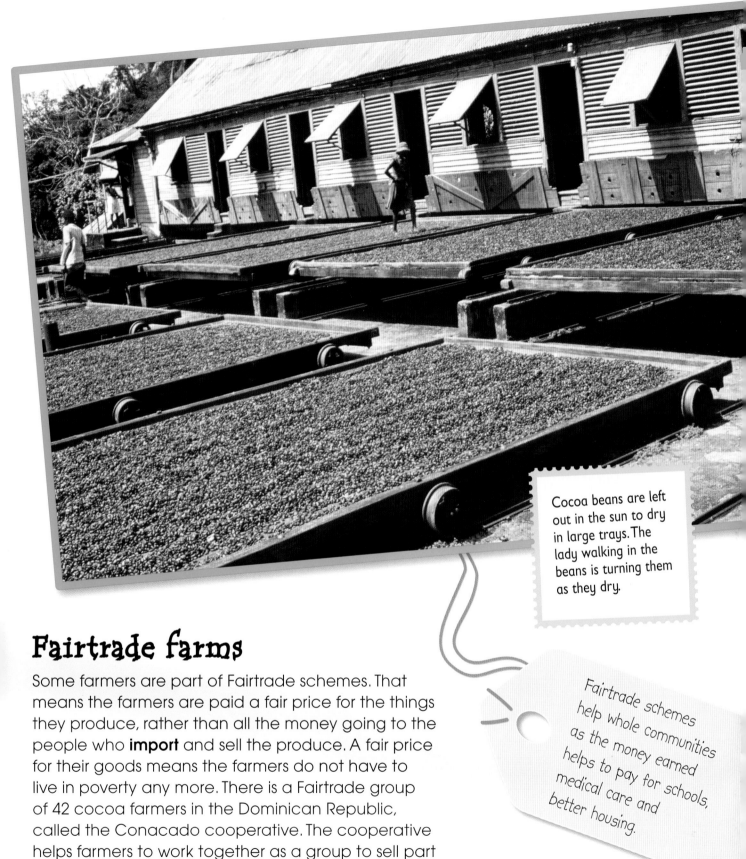

Cocoa beans are left out in the sun to dry in large trays. The lady walking in the beans is turning them as they dry.

Fairtrade farms

Some farmers are part of Fairtrade schemes. That means the farmers are paid a fair price for the things they produce, rather than all the money going to the people who **import** and sell the produce. A fair price for their goods means the farmers do not have to live in poverty any more. There is a Fairtrade group of 42 cocoa farmers in the Dominican Republic, called the Conacado cooperative. The cooperative helps farmers to work together as a group to sell part of its crop to the Fairtrade market. The farmers receive a guaranteed minimum price for their goods, and a bonus which is spent on the whole community.

Fairtrade schemes help whole communities as the money earned helps to pay for schools, medical care and better housing.

Food and drink

Caribbean food includes lots of fish caught in the warm waters of the Caribbean, and the delicious fruits and vegetables that grow in the hot, tropical climate.

Favourite dishes

Ackee and salt fish is the national dish of Jamaica and is often eaten for breakfast. It looks a bit like scrambled egg and is made of salt fish (fish preserved in salt), ackee, onions, tomatoes, peppers and pork fat all mixed up together. Ackee is a fruit that has many poisonous parts, so this dish is prepared very carefully. Another popular Caribbean dish is 'jerk' – chicken or pork slow-cooked over a flame. It is said to have begun when Maroons, escaped Jamaican slaves, cooked meat over open fires. Jerk uses peppers, pimento seeds, thyme and nutmeg for flavour and is cooked over hot coals covered with the branches of pimento or allspice wood.

Today for lunch I had my favourite food from a Shark & Bake stand – fried bakes, which are like thick, fried pancakes, filled with spicy shark meat – incredible! It beats sandwiches any day!
Love,
Kit

Callaloo and fungi

You'll find this dish in the Virgin Islands. Callaloo is like spinach soup or stew and it is cooked with crabs, **okra** and hot pepper sauce. Fungi has nothing to do with mushrooms, which you might expect. It is cornmeal and looks a bit like couscous or rice. It is served with callaloo to soak up the juices.

Sugar cane

Sugar cane is grown in the Caribbean. The sugar drips out of it as a kind of syrup. You can cut off the top of a cane and suck out the syrup. The local people use it to make cakes, pies and sweet fried dumplings as well as rum cake – a sponge soaked with rum.

Sugar cane used to be grown on large **plantations**. All the work was done by slaves. Today, sugar cane is grown for use by local people as well as to be made into sugar for export.

17

Island history

The Arawak, Carib and Taino Indians lived in the Caribbean long before Europeans arrived on the islands. They are now known as the **First Peoples**. The Arawak Indians were the first people that Christopher Columbus met when he came to the Caribbean. He landed on the island now called the Bahamas. These **indigenous** people were treated harshly by the explorers and settlers who came to the Caribbean, and many of them died.

This traditional windmill is on an old plantation on the Caribbean island of St Croix.

These ancient paintings were made by Arawak people. They are in the Fontein Cave in the Aruba Arikok National Park.

The First People

If you visit the Caribbean, you can see many museums that tell the story of the First People. In Jamaica, you can visit the Coyaba River Garden Museum in Ocho Rios, the Arawak Museum and the White Marl Taino Museum, in Kingston. You can also visit the Green Grotto Caves where you can see preserved cave drawings. In Cuba, you can see Arawak remains in the Montane Museum.

Historical buildings

There are also lots of buildings built by the invaders and settlers who **colonized** the Caribbean, such as the English, Spanish, Dutch and French. You can see churches and cathedrals, ruined fortifications, plantation houses and burial grounds.

This beautiful cathedral, Catedral de San Cristóbal de La Habana, was built in Havana in 1724.

I have been finding out all about the Taino people, some of the First People who lived in the Caribbean. I was amazed to discover that the Spanish explorers who came to the Bahamas, Cuba and Hispaniola in 1492 were all men. They had children with Taino women and many people in the Caribbean are descended from the First People.
Marlee

Terrible history

Across the Caribbean, African slaves were brought by the white settlers to work on their huge farms, called plantations. They lived terrible lives and were treated very badly. There are many people living in the Caribbean today who are descendents of those slaves. The slaves influenced the language, religion and festivals of the Caribbean today, bringing African traditions to the islands.

Pirates of the Caribbean

From the 1500s to the 1700s, the Caribbean was a haven for pirates, with thousands of coves and bays to hide in and even whole 'pirate towns' in which to spend their treasure! For example, the island of Tortuga was a pirate hideout for many years until around 1688. Pirate raids were carried out on Spanish ships as they moored off Cuba on their way to Spain.

Perfect for pirates

New Providence, in the Bahamas, was another pirate stronghold in the 1670s. It had a shallow harbour that pirate ships could travel into safely, but which was too small for warships to follow. The **trade lanes** between Europe and the West Indies, offered rich pickings for pirates as they plundered ships and then sailed away to hide in the many coves and bays. Many famous pirates visited the Bahamas, such as Blackbeard, Calico Jack Rackham and Anne Bonney.

Fort Fincastle in Nassau was built in 1793. It was a look-out point to protect the island from pirates.

Kidnapped!

If you go to Santiago de Cuba, you can visit the Piracy Museum in the Morro Castle. It is a fortress built in the 17th century high on a cliff over the bay. Between 1538 and 1562 Santiago de Cuba was the victim of terrible pirate attacks. The pirate Jacques de Sores attacked the city in the middle of the night, kidnapping people and holding them to ransom. The townsfolk decided they'd had enough and moved to Bayamo, away from the coast.

El Castillo del Morro (the Morro Castle) was built from 1539, by Spanish settlers to guard the entrance to San Juan bay from pirates and enemy ships.

 YOU'VE GOT MAIL

At school, we did a project on Port Royal. My class went on a pirate trail. I dressed up as Anne Bonney, the fierce pirate. I learned how the pirates fought with cutlasses – sharp swords. My friend Alex dressed as Blackbeard and even had a big false beard!
Love Sonia

Tourism

The Caribbean is a hugely popular holiday destination for visitors from all over the world. In particular, there are many tourists from North America, which is very close to the Caribbean.

Global warming is making sea temperatures rise, and coral reefs are dying as a result.

Eco tourism

Eco tourism describes holidays to beautiful, natural places, such as forests and beaches, where the tourists try to protect the places they are visiting. This is becoming popular in the Caribbean, with its rich and varied landscapes and wildlife. Many people come to the Caribbean to visit the beaches, and enjoy scuba diving on coral reefs. You can see **marlin**, porpoises, sharks and sea turtles as well as tiny, colourful reef fish. You may like to book a boat trip to watch huge, gentle whales swim by. Some people come for longer working holidays to help on environmental projects to preserve wildlife and animal habitats. You can also go on rainforest tours, staying in **eco lodges**, and trekking out into the jungle, watching brightly coloured birds in the **canopy**.

You must never touch the coral on a reef or it will be damaged and die.

Cruising the seas

Caribbean cruises are very popular luxury holidays, as they give travellers the chance to explore a variety of islands in one holiday. Many large cruise liners begin their Caribbean voyages from the southern end of North America. The ships are like floating hotels, with restaurants, discos, shops, gyms, spas, play areas and swimming pools.

Many tourists visit Turtle Beach in the town of Ochos Rios, Jamaica.

Do you like the photo of the bug on this postcard? It's a leaf-cutter ant. We saw them marching along vines in the rainforest in Costa Rica. They were carrying pieces of leaf much bigger than themselves. I also loved the spider monkeys that leapt backwards and forwards across the vines above our lodge, but they were really noisy! Our guide said we should be careful not to wear yellow – because not only does yellow attract insects but it also makes the monkeys likely to spray you with wee. I wore my blue T-shirt!
Jamie

A leaf-cutter ant colony can contain up to eight million ants!

Festivals and holidays

The Caribbean has many festivals and holidays, because settlers from lots of different places have brought their traditions with them. However, all the celebrations have a few things in common – colour, fun and great food!

Junkanoo is a street festival held in the Bahamas on 26 December and 1 January.

Carnival

All over the Caribbean Carnival, Carnaval or Carnavale is celebrated in spring. It began as a Christian festival at the beginning of Lent, the period that leads up to Easter. Today, massive celebrations are held, with parades, decorated floats, **steel pan drums** and street dancing. One of the best things about Carnival is the amazing costumes. Some of them have huge frames, made by bending wire and canes into all sorts of shapes, such as butterfly wings. The frames are covered in fabric, paper, plastic and, of course, lots of glitter and sequins. Many of the costumes are huge, but the person wearing the costume still needs to be able to dance!

Steel pan drums are traditionally made from the huge barrels that contained oil.

People spend months making the beautiful costumes they wear at Carnival time.

I can't believe that it's nearly time for Carnival again. Only three weeks now – I can't wait! Mum has been making the wings for my butterfly costume for months – she's sewn on loads of sequins. She's going as a black widow spider. She looks brilliant, but Dad's a bit worried!
love
Betty x

Saut d'Eau

In Haiti, there is a festival called Saut d'Eau. Saut d'Eau is a well and waterfall where it is believed that an image of the Virgin Mary appeared in the 1800s. Today, many **pilgrims** pray to the Voudoun goddess of love – Erzulie. People walk a long way to visit the waterfall, where they bathe in the waters as drummers play music. There is a feast, and prayers are said.

Environmental issues

The Caribbean has many fabulous natural resources, from crystal clear water and beautiful cloud forests to rainforests teeming with animal life. This attracts visitors who want to experience all the beauty first-hand, but that can cause problems. The more visitors who want to come, the more likely it is that the environment will be damaged. If there are more tourists, more hotels, resorts and facilities need to be built to accommodate them.

Widespread destruction

All this development can lead to the destruction of animal habitats and pollution. Many Caribbean islands are taking steps to protect their wildlife and habitats, and there are many national parks full of animals and plants such as passion flowers, orchids and hibiscus. The British Virgin Islands has 17 protected national parks, including St Eustatius Marine Park which has protected areas for endangered leatherback turtles to lay eggs.

These black-necked stilts enjoy protection in the Palo Verde National Park, in Costa Rica.

Threatened birds

Protection is important because many plant and animal species that live in the Caribbean are very rare. In Dominica, scientists are studying the nesting behaviour of threatened Sisserou and Jaco parrots to see what needs to be done to protect them. In Jamaica and the Cayman Islands, the Buffy Flower bat is studied so that they may be protected in the future.

Saving the fish

Marine life in the Caribbean is also protected by not allowing too many fish to be caught for food. Coral reefs and the creatures that live there are protected against being taken from the sea to be sold to tourists as souvenirs.

The Imperial parrot is only found in the mountain rainforest of Dominica and is protected from hunters by law.

Leatherback turtles live their whole life – which can be as long as 80 years – at sea. Females return to land only to lay their eggs.

I have been studying the Las Baulas National Park on the Pacific coast of Costa Rica. It is where rare leatherback turtles come to nest and lay their eggs. The turtles are counted, and the nests are protected from predators. The beaches are patrolled and guarded to stop people stealing the eggs and scaring the turtles.
Paul

Activity ideas

1 Look at websites about the Caribbean. Make a list of twenty of the islands you find, and a fact about each one.

2 Using books and the Internet, find out about the creatures that live on coral reefs in the Caribbean. Make a fact file about the plants and creatures who live in and around the reefs.

3 Imagine that you are travelling through the Caribbean. How will you travel? By cruise ship, by sea plane or maybe by bike? What will you see? Write a journal about your trip.

4 Find out about carnival costumes and masks. Design and make your own mask from thin card, decorated with feathers and sequins.

5 Find out more about hurricanes. Write an explanation abut how hurricanes are formed.

6 Find recordings of music by reggae artists, such as Bob Marley. While you are listening to the music, paint or draw a bright picture of a sunny Caribbean beach.

7 Plan a holiday to the Caribbean. Which islands would you visit? Which sites would you go and see? Use the Internet and travel brochures to help you plan your trip.

8 Find out more about the Arawak, Carib and Taino people – the First People of the Caribbean. Describe what happened to them when invaders and settlers, such as the Spanish, English and Dutch, arrived.

9 Make a model of a leatherback turtle. Stuff a paper bag with cotton wool for the body, and make the legs and head from card. Tape them onto the bag. Then make a shell from crumpled brown and green crêpe paper stuck onto a round card base. Glue the shell to your turtle's body. You could make white tissue or clay eggs, too!

10 Write a story about a leatherback turtle fighting her way ashore to lay her eggs. What dangers does she face? Imagine you are the turtle – what are your feelings? What will happen to your eggs when you return to the sea?

11 With a grown-up, visit the supermarket and make a list of all the Fairtrade food that is available. Buy some Fairtrade chocolate, and 'taste test' to see how it compares with ordinary brands.

NOTE FOR ADULTS: Please ensure that children do not suffer from any food allergies before carrying out a taste test.

12 Find out more about what life was like for the African people taken to work on plantations in the Caribbean. Research using books in your school library.

13 Find a Caribbean folk tale from a book or the Internet. Read it, and then draw illustrations for the story. You could get togther with some friends and perform the folk tale as a play.

14 Write a leaflet for tourists describing Kingston, Jamaica. Use exciting language so that people are encouraged to visit.

15 Make your own pirate treasure chest. Get an old shoebox and attach the back of the lid to the back of the box with tape to make a hinge. Tape a rectangle of card to the lid, curved over to make it look like a proper pirate treasure chest. Cover the box in a few layers of strips of newspaper glued with PVA glue. When your chest has dried, paint it brown and draw on 'studs' with a gold pen. Fill it with your pirate treasure!

16 Find a recipe for callalloo in a recipe book or on the Internet. With a grown-up, try making the dish. If you cannot find all the ingredients for the dish, ask an adult to help you to adapt it.

NOTE FOR ADULTS: Please ensure that children do not suffer from any food allergies before making or eating any food.

17 Carry out research using the Internet, magazines and newspapers to find out more about the problem of water pollution on reefs in the Caribbean. Use the information you find to design a leaflet to tell people about the dangers to the environment.

18 Imagine you are a pirate. Write a journal of your adventures – and don't forget to describe the treasure you find!

19 Look at old pirate maps in books or on the Internet. Age a piece of paper by painting it with tea or coffee and crumpling it up a few times to make it look old. Draw a map complete with islands, treasure and sea monsters. Complete the map with a blob of red wax crayon melted on the corner as a seal – press an old pen lid into the soft wax to make an imprint.

Glossary

archipelago A large group of islands.

artefacts Objects of historical interest, such as tools, weapons or ornaments .

biodiversity Lots of different plant and animal species found in an environment.

canopy The top level of a rainforest.

Christopher Columbus An Italian explorer living in the 1400s who worked for the Spanish kings and queen.

climate The usual weather conditions of a particular place or region.

cloud forests Tropical forests, often near peaks of coastal mountains, which have cloud cover all year.

cocoa Powder made from the seeds of the cacao plant, used in making chocolate.

colonized To take over and make your own.

Conservation International A group concerned with looking after the planet.

crops Plants or agricultural produce.

eco lodges Places where tourists stay, which are friendly to the environment.

export Shipping goods to sell in other countries.

First People People who are native to a particular place.

hurricanes Violent tropical storms.

hydrofoils Boats that travel across the water very fast by skimming over the surface.

import To bring in goods from another country to sell.

indigenous People, animals or plants that originated in a particular place or country.

mangrove A tropical tree that grows in mud and swamps.

marlin A large game fish.

merengue A ballroom dance from Dominica and Haiti.

okra A small, green vegetable, also called ladies' fingers.

peninsula An area of land almost completely surrounded by water, except it is connected to the mainland.

pilgrims People who go on a journey to visit a place for religious reasons.

plantations Large farms that used slave labour to produce cotton, sugar and other crops

reggae A type of music popular across the Caribbean, especially in Jamaica.

regional Relating to a particular place or region.

salsa A fast ballroom dance, originally from Puerto Rica.

schooners Sailing ships with two or more masts.

steel pan drum Bowl-shaped percussion instruments common in the Caribbean, made from steel barrels.

trade lanes Routes taken by ships to transport goods from place to place.

tropical Hot and humid climate.

Index